Outside the Big-Paned Windows

Outside the Big-Paned Windows

Poems by

Greg Maddigan

Cover by Shay Culligan
Cover Art by Abigail Maddigan

ISBN: 978-1-63980-078-0

Kelsay Books
502 South 1040 East, A-119
American Fork, Utah 84003
Kelsaybooks.com

For Stacy

Acknowledgments

Grateful acknowledgment is made to the editors of the publications listed below, where the following poems first appeared:

The Bookends Review: "Reeling Still"

The Cortland Review: "On the Water with My Mother"

Grey Sparrow Journal: "At Mission San Buenaventura with My Son"

The Legendary: "Gold Finches," "Prehistoric"

Panoplyzine: "Generations Heeling"

SHIFT: "A Schizophrenic Lover Talks to God," "Ten Thousand Difficulties"

Tipton Poetry Journal: "God Shed His Grace"

Tule Review: "In this Backyard Tent"

Wilderness House Literary Review: "At Skip Rock Bay," "Rounding Anacapa with My Father"

2 Bridges Review: "Such Wise Men"

Contents

On the Water with My Mother

Unexpectedly,
pelicans.
They arrive in untamed formations, celestial
accordions, from the green refuges of the deep west.
They rise and fall on
air drafts, like the unseen levers of the past
that move our conversations.
We both wonder how it might have been different had
you stayed.
Maybe, in all the after-years, all we needed
was to share this little canoe, to glide through the soft weeping
marshes, listening to the pelicans winging.
Their white feathers, tips
dipped in black like our consciences,
play the music
of our gaping wonder.
We half-expect the birds to turn into
silken handkerchiefs, or red plastic roses, or warm white rabbits
pulled from the blue sleeve of sky.
But instead they drift up the valley
to the north,
like forgiveness,
right before our very eyes.

God Shed His Grace

We wake up in the night now
Alone, always, under the star-spackled sky.
We are wind-milling and tilting again.
We are post-solstice.
We know we have wasted
Our time; we want to weep or
Punch someone in the larynx.
How unexceptional.
We plead for our star to return, for
Someone, anyone
To make us great again.

Instead, there is only a mandarin slice
Of melancholic moon;
Still, we long to wade into its
Nostalgic light.

In the morning, the fog clings
To the paint-flecked front porches of America.
The basalt landscape rises out of the Columbia,
Out of our constitution,
Like a newborn foal, still steaming from its inception.
If only Jefferson could see the place now.

The wheat barges come and go,
And we talk of the new casino.
Vineyards quilt the slopes beyond the northern bank,
And we talk with faces white and blank.
We wonder: will we know when any given supper
Will be our last?

Above the dam,
The American flag hangs limp on its pole.
Soon, the spring winds will rustle it
So full of patriotism
The Stars and Stripes will be in tatters.
In town,
The televisions light up every living room.
They are all blaring; we can't stop watching even though
We know we are in the throes of our own
Asphyxiation, our final flickering.

We wonder if we should just go back to sleep,
Or maybe we ought to go
Buy a gun.
We gaze to the onion fields in the east, harrowed and
Soon to be seeded with sweet bulbs, then shivering with scissoring
Green stalks beneath a dawn-yawning pink sky
Tumultuously untangling itself from rumbling
Thunderheads.
We hop in the pick-up
And drive out to the unhappy hills,
The ones freckled with sagebrush,
Furrowed by hard work and hunger.
We stop the truck and unfold our bodies,
Wrinkled origami figurines, crinkled and cast
Aside on an American roadside.
The barbed wire fences catch our desperate dreams
Like tumbleweeds.
Our worries crowd the branches of our minds
Like the immigrant Starlings roosting in the
Winter Cottonwoods.

Maybe we should occupy a wildlife refuge.
Maybe we should accept
That we will float, then plummet from the sky
Like the birds teeming on the Pacific Flyway.

Night will fall on the land.
The moon will be up in dry dock.
We will sleep like wolves,
Waking in the ragged night,
Turning circles around ourselves.
We will awaken again to the inaugural yapping of the
Coyotes, heralding our fear
Of the dark.
Nevertheless, we stamp our boots in the dirt.
Even in winter,
This air smells like onions.

7 Hours at Carpinteria Beach

1.
We are seventeen and we stumble
through the chaparral to the low bluff
just in time to see the Easter
sky tumble into the water
like oranges poured from a whiskey
barrel.

2.
She leans her temple on the bone
chapel of my scapula. The
cymbal sun crashes upon the
staves of the waves. Her pink finger
tends to mine, a crosier in the
tambourine light. The shorebreak longs
to steam upon the tawny sand.

She tells me she will put her tent
next to mine. Her ribboning hair
brushes the archipelago
of my worth.

3.
We watch spindrift from the breakers,
set alight, a Buddhist monk's robe,
unraveling our intentions.

My words brush the auricle of
her ear: I will be waiting for
you. The Pacific wind wraps us
up, a giant conch.

4.
At night, by the bonfire, we
burn driftwood and innuendo.
We sit apart, listening to
the great swells unrolling along
the tar bluffs, measuring each glance
and the distance the mournful loon
traveled to issue its chorus,
a tremolo call to us from
the cresting tide beneath the night
pier.

5.
In the amber lantern tent, set
in this soft bower of purple
needle grass, beneath the high bright
track of Herculean milk, I
am invincible, eternal;
our virgin minds twine, braiding in
to infinity, our fill of
bliss on bliss.

6.
I wake up alone, wishing for
the remnant warmth of her caged ribs,
her clavicle. Now, the whole world
lies before me, and the predawn
dark swallows me, a deep inky
sepulcher throat.

7.
The tatters of my idealism
smolder beneath my Mexican
poncho. All that remains is the
steep cliff to the beach plain and the
cannoning sea, echoing its
arcane wisdom endlessly in
the guilty fog.

postscript
Sometimes, usually in winter's
strained and stained-glass solstice light, a
fragment of Indian paintbrush
and poppy sunset, I recall
nestling with her and observing
the frothy coupling of the land
and sea, bones in a pale pine box.

Resting my head on my anti-
septic pillow, I sense her sharp
citrus smell, the summer globes
in the Valencia groves on
Highway 126, her words,
whispering like the elegant
wind-lifted long-legged seabirds,
and like every other damn
thing, ascending to the stricken
and unintelligible sky.

Generations Heeling

Foreword
Our parents' voices have been swallowed
by the earth. Their wishes for us are still
with them, clanking against the backs of their cold teeth.
We can no longer know
what they almost confided in us,
what we desperately wanted to hear,
what was always just behind the gates of their
lips.
We look upon what they have
left us
and realize that the end is

I.
Everywhere:
in the trembling underbelly of the pressing storm;

in the topographical map of our skin, the years
etched there indelibly, thickening our tolerance for
disappointment;

in our families, the generations heeling like
boats on the loyal tides—riding the keel
between the sea stacks and the clamming beds, tacking between
the sand dollar beaches and the remote reefs,
swinging wildly between love and guilt, mast lines jangling
like church bells, sails luffing and blown full—
we wait for the bottom to blow holes in
our exhilaration;

in the glittering yellow leaves
tumbling like lost dreams
through the back alleys of our lantern-lit minds—

II.

Everywhere. In the funereal afternoons, we sit in mothballed
rooms watching
the bark unravel on our bony branches.
The tight feeling in our joints
presages
the cold prick of winter's coming needle:
the hearses leaving churches
on lonely weekday

III.

Mornings. In the evenings, the rooms become cloistered like
coffins so we step outside and run
our hands through our hair
in the brittle breeze and
clumps fall

IV.

Out. At night, on these empty front porches,
the air is redolent with rain
and the smell of their closets, their sheets.
We wince, close our eyes, and see
the sunsets of our youth
weeping impossible light
onto the swollen hills
of our idealism, our naivete.
We remember believing in perfection:
the green oxbow in the river
where the salmon pooled up like rippling ecstasy;
the chaotic clusters of the grape arbor;
the gentle lapping of the waves
on the shores of our imaginations;

our parents' pedestals;
the benefit of toil, the way it tore away
the detritus of hurt;
the downy hair of infants, tufting out from
misshapen heads;
and love.
We peer into the darkness
from these slouching and weather-beaten platforms,
from the abandoned monasteries of our lives.
We cross ourselves relentlessly while
life clatters all around us—we are
smeared with the whorling imprints of
privation and

V.

Bliss. At midnight, after the wine and the festivals of the human
heart, we are content, maybe even ebullient,
to be lost in the undertow
of each other.
We know that in the morning we will be glad
for another cup of coffee.

Afterword
We have reached a detente with
their dusty voices, their silence,
with our orphaned regret.
Maybe next time
we will give what is so
desperately needed from us.

The whining world tries to drown out their wisdom:
don't you want to live forever?
Instead, we steady our palsied souls
and stumble on
towards the sacred.

Reeling Still

What I wouldn't give
for another morning like that one:

I brought you Kona coffee and sunny-side-up eggs,
pausing momentarily at the bedroom door,
teak tray perched on my fingertips, to watch
you float on the rippling blue comforter,
a still life, swimming a statuesque side-stroke.
The birds in the branches outside
our bedroom window capered about in the yellow-breasted
sunlight.
The maple tree, wrapped in wet brown bark,
sprouted buds
bejeweled by last night's fog—
the same little beads which slid down
your naked skin in the shower,
dawn after presumptive dawn.

I sip my coffee alone now, in the first anodyne rays
of the mourning hours, measuring my life
in birdsong—plaintive and palliative.

At Skip Rock Bay

We are staring at the big empty bay, listening to a susurrus move
through the cattails and reeds behind us, watching a heron
poised on a pointed tree top like a Tai Chi master.
We realize that we have never been here before

without the children—a decade, at least, since their little fingers
wrapped so readily around these flat beach rocks, these smooth,
soothing stones before flinging them
wildly upon the waters.

Every rock, teal and marbled by memory,
the concentrated color of a thousand earths, a thousand childhoods,
skips, careening like the years,
away from us.

Now, we sit in a bed of fossils,
bleached evidence of our old ties, our spent days, our heroic tales
of circumnavigating the sun;
there is no one left to listen.

I hurl a rock, this one mottled red with my regrets, the color of the
sun setting in fire season, born from the forge of a distant artist
with callous hands and crow's feet
and a sometimes callous heart.

I wish we could ride a skipped rock, beyond
the coffin flatness of the horizon's tight lid, into next year,
and the year after that, skimming
the water's skin, together.

Gold Finches

Two
Gold
Finches
Re-
splend-
ent,
Re-
volv-
ing
A-
round
Seeds,
Peck-
ing
The
Future,
Dangl-
ing
And
Spinn-
ing
From
Twine,
Male
And
Female,
Be-
neath
The
Lilac
Branches
Un-
der

The
Spent
Blooms
Be-
hind
The
Lattice
Of
Late
Summer.

At Mission San Buenaventura with My Son

We duck out of the rain, into the adobe vacancy.
We blink back images from the frivolous pier, the floating
fireworks runnelled on the flipsides of our eyelids.
My son's flip-flops irreverently slap the hard floor, little
sound waves lapping at the base of the Crucifix, the wood wrung
from the velvet foothills, riveted with iron strong enough to
suspend a grown man, like the sun, by the wrists and shattered
lower leg bones above the earth for hours, for eternity. My son's
nonchalance echoes all the way to Eden. We coast
down the middle aisle, a wake between the wood,
genuflecting before the heavy centuries.

What did the Chumash think when St. Serra disciplined
their wild souls?
I envy their rebellion, their need to
burn driftwood in the sand, to carve their longings
in the sea bluffs, to rattle and chant under the basilica sky,
to dance, limbs disploding into light,
to get and spend on the things that matter.
My son is a wild soul; I wonder what he wonders, his coltish knees
spancelled by the kneeler, corralled by the pew.

Back outside, crossed and holy-watered, I glance over my
shoulder, relieved to see my son
gambol into the marbled light of the Mission Garden.
He says, "I could have stayed
inside
forever."
At whose command would I tie my son to such an altar?

Prehistoric

I have seen you
In the early morning
Stealing through the forest
With your prehistoric longings
Your pterodactyl heritage
Your ancient tenure, your skittish rafter.
I have seen you
With your tail spread wide like a Japanese fan,
Like my optimism for the day.

I have seen your jaunty strut
Your wrinkled neck
Bright with the fury
Of survival, colored with
The capriciousness of emotion:
Of joy, envy, love, and a sometimes tiny head, tiny heart.

I have heard you
Calling me from my dreams
With your raucous gobble
Your gossiping followed by
Laughter laughter laughter.
I know you,
So imperfect, so beautiful.

Such Wise Men

We have traveled a long way for nothing.
This was supposed to be different.
We expected the hard-knotted pews, the sky cracking open
like our eyelids at birth, the splinters in our fingers from carrying
such a heavy burden. We believed what we were told.
It was supposed to be radiant,
like the acclaim we desired, like the moon rising over
the empty barns, the rolling shepherds' hills, the corpses of
Calvary. It was supposed to be salvific.

All we ever wanted was to be beckoned,
to hear the sound of our names from the stone altars, from deep
inside the hushed woods, to be a child leaping for joy in the womb.
We have misplaced our faith again.

We thought by now we would have stumbled upon
a satisfactory stable, or three trees on the low sky.
We thought by now the women would have come
running from the tomb. Instead, we are road-sore and thirsty,
laid up in mean-spirited roadhouses, night after night.
And now we are locked in this upper room
with our cowardice. Herod slaughters the innocents in our heads;
Pilate washes his hands in our hearts. No bright gardener has said
to us, Why do you seek the living among the dead?
If only we could have blood on our hands; instead,
folly is packed tightly beneath our fingernails.

We wait and watch the snow fall like our disappointments, the
heavy flakes floating through the empty branches of our lives.
We wish the birds would come back.
We wish the night fires would remain lit, that the star would
appear, but we are stuck clutching our brokenness,
our galled, sore-footed, refractory selves.

A Schizophrenic Lover Talks to God

I.

I plunk stones into the slack waters of my Identity
and the ripples give me Anxiety because instead of thinking of me,
I am thinking of you, your head cocked just so, your fingers
lingering on the page. I know the seasons change the way we both
think, yet the earth still spins like a loom, a dancer who only
knows one move. We both fear we are slipping with her tilt, pall-
born away with white flowers and white gloves. We can't tell what
matters anymore. Maybe these Words themselves contain our
matter, like the filigree of some ancient text we long to believe.
How can we have rotated the sun more than thirty-three times
and still know so little?

II.

One of us will always want to claim clarity.
In the beginning was The Word.
The Word tented among us, sat beneath a tree, radiant,
King of our migrant hearts. The Word made me euphoric and You
melancholic, me guilty and You compassionate, Me saintly and
You extravagant. I want to recite the old knowledge from rote
memory. You want to ask the daunting and absurd questions.
You want to kneel. I want to fly.
I want to knead the rosary beads. You want to contemplate the river
flowing endlessly.
Can we do this, together?

III.

The summer thunder jars my awe and your
nostalgia for the Garden. Beneath the rain, the forest life—
the inchworm inching, the velvety buck bedding down in the itchy
grass with flies on his pupils, the songbirds mobbing the Pygmy
Owl on the low branch—moves to a rhythm, as if we don't matter,

as if we will never matter. No wonder we envy the Cormorants,
compasses oriented to the sun, faces streaked yellow, never unsure,
sitting in a patient line on a log beneath the emerald slope of the
mountains. On cloudy days, they wait for a revelation, eyeing
the Grebes' nests, grassy circles in the water, ringed holiday
wreaths foretelling glad tidings which the Cormorants seem to

already know.
You would be a Cormorant if you could,
stubbornly waiting to matter. To me.

IV.
These Words matter, coalescing in the air
between my mouth and your ear canal.
Your lips are a conch, a secret we share. I know you…
the hope in your heart, your bleak dawns, your pettiness, your
brilliance, your longings, your agony in the garden.
I want to walk down tree bark with You, with the confidence
and certainty of dripping sap.
We will crack seeds in the dark crevices. I want to share our
confidences, but they only brook-babble about in my head,
gibberish. The same for You, I am sure. I can only peck at the
Truth.

V.
I float on coffee, thinking of You, creating galactic halos
with skipped rocks. The water's surface is mysterious,
a skin, your skin, God's skin. I listen to the applause of thunder,
the gobbling of turkeys, and wait for darkness to wash over
the land like sweet-grass smoke. Maybe You will stay with me.
Or are You getting ready to leave?
Either way, I can be sure of what I have always suspected:

the bats are roosting in the archways between my teeth;
the stealthy coal trains are ushering the earth away from us
with soothing midnight whistles; I will never stand on a piling
drying my wet wings like a karate sensei.

VI.
How I wish I were
paddling in a Cottonwood
blizzard with You.
But You already knew that,
Didn't You?
Meet me at the boat launch
past the old railroad
Trestle, or are You
there
Already?

Rounding Anacapa with My Father

The Santa Barbara Channel floats before us,
horizon to horizon, like falling petals of blue Iris—
the generosity of the sea at dawn.
The Channel Islands bob in the distance,
buoys of our shared past with water:
I remember the way
You heeled the Sunflower at Castaic Lake until
I was certain that I would pitch headlong into
the marbled blue-green iris of
the impenetrable future.
You would not let us capsize, with just the two of us
left on the lake.

The knifing hull of the catamaran rounds Anacapa, laying a wake:
past the battered cliffs, the adolescent fury of the open waves,
past the Fin and Blue Whales, shiny backs black in the crashing
sunlight, past the white-spotted rookeries, the jagged rock arch.
On the way back to the Ventura docks:
Dolphins, two thousand or more,
nosing, somersaulting, chirping, clicking, clowning, whistling—
acrobats of the absurd.
They echo-locate off my ecstasy.
Your whooping exhilaration blows joy
into the sails of my
tomorrow.

We sit at the fishermen's bar at the end of the day,
and I know how this will end, the same as always,
the silence louder than the clattering cutlery.
We are men. We are engulfed by the words
none of us want to say
but all of us want to hear.

After our time together,
I can ease back
into the darkness outside the big-paned windows,
knowing that in the harbor,
all the boats
are still floating.

At Mission Santa Barbara with My Daughter

My teenaged daughter points to the
shadow of the cross splintering
the red tiled roof like the bristle-
brush wings of a roosting beady-
black egret. Regret and roses
the size of beating hearts bloom
in my ribcage beneath the worn
bell tower.

Inside, the dark is cool like dirt by
the shovelful. From the nave, I
can't help but see the Chumash queued
in the garden's furrowed rows, blue
uniforms buckled over to
pile the soil like ashes
from an oven. They chant non-sense.
Work prescribed for salvation.

I am buckled over with them.
I wish my daughter could see them,
too, but she is kneeling beneath
the wracked body, her fingers
templed against her smooth temple.
I am no Abraham. I wish
another life for her. We go
outside, anointed by the luke-

warm water and the tidal breeze.
A spring cloudburst pock-marks the pools,
puddles boiled up like smallpox
on the backs of the Chumash. Soon,

she will see them, too. Now, she sees
only the bay and the holy
blue. I would move tombstones for her,
if I could.

In this Backyard Tent

How surprising
to be awakened by
a pileated woodpecker,
Tap-tap-tapping
the green silence, extracting
beetle larvae for the nestling brood,
hopping from hollow to
hollow.

He drums a meditation, a Taize prayer:
the colorful tapping of flapping flags, of flapping years,
of my always present children, now gone, beating their arms
like the wings of the great fall migrations,
shushing each other while bird watching
with high resolution binoculars
fashioned from empty toilet paper rolls.
Hair sticking up. Smiles off-kilter. Years off-kilter.
I unzip the tent, letting the morning's washed light
dodder like dust particles in the cluttered rooms of mid-life.
I listen for your floating anxiety, feathered and untethered, winging
away with your red crested head in the sadness of these whirring
woods. I worry I will fade into the unpeeling of another day.

The dark knuckled roots of the giant
trees splay out beneath me like the memories of births, like my
wife's hair on the white hospital pillow in the maternity ward.

Gethsemane Moon

That was the night I sat in a wicker
deck chair with eggplant lungs and watched the gold
monstrance of the pandemic moon proceed
through the incense air beneath the sooty
sky buttresses. That was the night her flour-
light clung to my panting breaths like cement.
My children know this moon, the frequent lead
protagonist in their bedtime stories
for an undervalued millennium.
I longed for enough oxygen to
tell one last tale. Maybe, I prayed, if
I closed my eyes, for just a crawling brown
caterpillar second, the moon might burst
from its cocoon, and waft away on wings,
polka-dotted yellow, carrying my
soul away with it, leaving only this
destitute carapace, and the backs of
my pear wood eyelids etched with the muted
figures of my small children imprinted
on a woodblock mountain, in snowy drifts.

A tranquil thought, but then a fevered red-
mercury rush: my children gathered near
a Lebanon cedar casket. I am
too young for this. I forbid this. There will
be no standing spade, no statuary
heron hunting a slough in a green field;
there will be no desiccated relic
exposed to the open aquarium
sky, no fish carcass nestled in this blue
pebble-gravel graveyard. I did not know
dying would involve such shame, unfettered

agony, at letting loved ones down, did
not know death was letting loved ones down. I
never realized I was subject to
Newton and depressing gravity, and
then, I feared black sleep: what if I had been
pretending the moon all along? Who would
loft such a cratered mess into the sky
every night for my children? What if,
without me, the Schrodinger moon would crack,
collapse—a broken lung, punctured by my
hubris, exhaling its final breath, in
solitude. Every final labored
breath rattles in solitude. That was the
night my friends slept, the night I sweat wet drops
of blood in Gethsemane, the night I
finally understood why Jesus wept.

Ten Thousand Difficulties

I am like them, a fisher of men, my faith
buoyed momentarily by bustling nets
sewn with pragmatic linen. I follow,
parceling out the loaves, waiting for my loyal moment,
my right hand seat. I am surprised
by the words of denial, centipedes' legs, skittering swiftly across
my firelit lips, chinking like silver coins in the wells of my ears:
Oh, these fissures of men.

At that first moment, though, by the foam and choppy water, I
walked away from my boat, one of the chosen, thinking
I will, he will, transubstantiate
my life.

Later, when I fell asleep in the garden, dreaming doubt—
Maybe I should have stayed home to
dance with my daughters, to
fling my son by his bony ankles into the deep waters, to
spoon my wife's naked body in the gloaming, to
gather up her garments, to
anoint her feet with oil, to
haul and mend, haul and mend.

Another Short Happy Life

The first time I saw You bare, You wore a
pearl necklace and a feathered bed. I was
eighteen. Much later, exhausted, after
work, and many births, and tiny daily
deaths, we met beneath the desperate fires
of the Chinese lanterns. The hushed, busy
waters beneath the wooden bridge gossiped
of our demise, but your tongue insisted
upon sunrises and boats heeling, sails
blown to bliss by your trade-wind lips. And now,

after decades of moving through the blue
risings with You, the fertile afternoons,
the ruddy sunsets over the scalloped
drifts of the ocean dunes, the bruised purple
chirping, You remain more beautiful than
the dawn hips of the bays, cradled by the
sloping Pacific hills, more beautiful
than our nativity star at its sheer
zenith, than waves curling up on tumbled
sundown beaches, washed hospital sheet white
by the forlorn moonlight. Please, just a few

more syllables.

In Memory of
Mrs. Shea

About the Author

Greg Maddigan lives in Spokane, Washington with his wife, Stacy. He attended Gonzaga University where he earned degrees in English and Religious Studies. He teaches at the On Track Academy. Greg is the author of the chapbook of poems, *Paddling through the Meridian's Wake* (Finishing Line Press). Greg's poetry has also appeared in the *Legendary,* the *Tipton Poetry Journal,* the *Cortland Review,* the *Wilderness House Literary Review,* the *Tule Review, Panoplyzine,* the *Grey Sparrow Journal,* the *Bookends Review,* and *SHIFT.* His work is forthcoming in the *2 Bridges Review.*